NATIVE NATIONS OF NORTH AMERICA

Life of the
NAVAJO

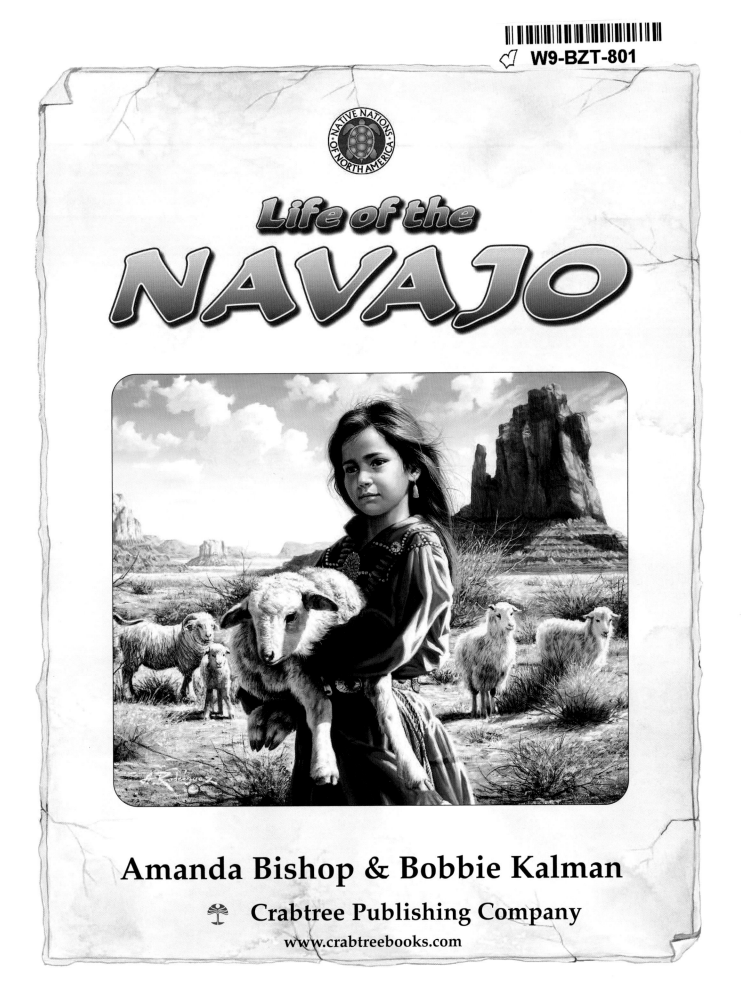

Amanda Bishop & Bobbie Kalman

Crabtree Publishing Company

www.crabtreebooks.com

Life of the
NAVAJO

Created by Bobbie Kalman

Dedicated by Amanda Bishop
For Dr. Paula Kot, a mentor and an inspiration

Editor-in-Chief
Bobbie Kalman

Writing team
Amanda Bishop
Bobbie Kalman

Substantive editor
Niki Walker

Editors
Rebecca Sjonger
Kathryn Smithyman

Art director
Robert MacGregor

Design
Katherine Berti

Production coordinator
Heather Fitzpatrick

Photo research
Crystal Sikkens
Laura Hysert

Consultants
Professor Herbert John Benally, Center for Diné Studies, Diné College
Dr. Maureen Trudelle Schwarz, Department of Anthropology, Maxwell
    School of Citizenship and Public Affairs, Syracuse University

Photographs and reproductions
Smithsonian American Art Museum, Washington, DC / Art Resource, NY: front cover,
    page 11 (top)
Courtesy of the Eiteljorg Museum of American Indians and Western Art: *Horizons of
    Yesterday*, Don Louis Perceval (image trimmed), page 8 (top); *In the Land of the Navajo*,
Robert Lougheed (image trimmed), page 20
James King (Navajo name: Woolenshirt): *Four Corners*, page 7; *Family Picking*, page 9;
    Storyteller, page 17
Nativestock.com: pages 16, 31 (top)
The Philbrook Museum of Art, Tulsa, Oklahoma: pages 11 (bottom), 19
Artwork from PicturesNow.com: pages 6, 23 (top), 25
Alfredo Rodriguez: *Navajo Wealth*, title page, back cover; *The Meeting Place*, page 5 (top);
    Navajo Patriarch, page 8 (bottom); *Navajo Family*, page 10; *Navajo Wedding*, pages 12-13;
    Sharing Secrets, page 14; *Navajo Goat Milk*, page 15; *Shearing Time*, page 21;
    Weaving Lesson, page 22
Arthur Shilstone: pages 28-29
Courtesy United States Mint. Used with permission: page 31 (bottom)
Charles D. Winters: page 30 (bottom)
Other images by Digital Stock and Circa:Art/Image Club Graphics

Illustrations
Barbara Bedell: pages 5, 18 (herbs, rabbit & maize), 21
Katherine Berti: border, pages 11, 12, 18 (snake), 24 (top)
Margaret Amy Salter: pages 4, 18 (wolf), 26 (bottom), 30
Bonna Rouse: pages 1 (background), 15, 16, 18 (beans & eagle), 24 (bottom), 26 (top)

Crabtree Publishing Company

www.crabtreebooks.com   1-800-387-7650

Printed in the USA/092015/CG20150812

Library of Congress Cataloging-in-Publication Data
Bishop, Amanda.
  Life of the Navajo / Amanda Bishop & Bobbie Kalman.
      p. cm. -- (Native nations of North America series)
Includes index.
Contents: The Navajo people--Harmony and respect--Navajo
communities--Family life--Marriage--The lives of children--At home in
a hogan -- Food from the land -- The importance of animals--Weaving--
Arts, crafts, and clothing--Dangerous times--Forcing change--The
Navajo today.
  ISBN 0-7787-0376-2 (RLB) -- ISBN 0-7787-0468-8(pbk.)
  1. Navajo Indians--History--Juvenile literature. 2. Navajo Indians--
Social life and customs--Juvenile literature. [1. Navajo Indians. 2.
Indians of North America--Southwest, New.]
I. Kalman, Bobbie. II. Title. III. Series.
E99.N3B5383 2004
979.1004'9726--dc22
                                                2003012912
                                                LC

**Published in
Canada
Crabtree Publishing**
616 Welland Ave.
St. Catharines, ON
L2M 5V6

**Published in the
United States
Crabtree Publishing**
PMB 59051
350 Fifth Avenue, 59th Floor
New York, New York 10118

**Published in the United
Kingdom
Crabtree Publishing**
Maritime House
Basin Road North, Hove
BN41 1WR

**Published in Australia
Crabtree Publishing**
3 Charles Street
Coburg North
VIC, 3058

Contents

The Navajo people

The people of the Navajo **nation** call themselves *Diné*, or "People." The Navajo homeland, shown below, is in the Southwest region of the United States. It is called the *Diné Bikéyah*, which means "among the people." The Navajo people have lived in the Southwest for hundreds of years. Many **archaeologists**, or scientists who study ancient cultures, believe that the **ancestors** of the Navajo journeyed south from present-day Canada. They probably arrived in the Southwest sometime between 1000 and 1400. The people were **nomadic hunter-gatherers** who survived by moving from place to place in search of animals to hunt and plants to gather. They spoke an Athabascan language.

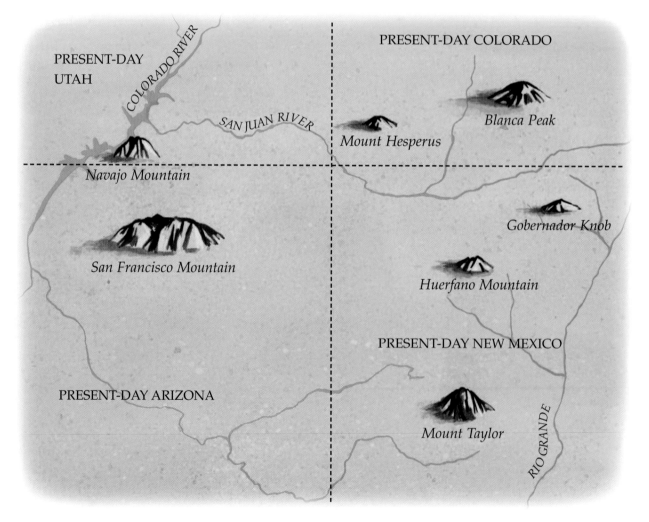

The Diné Bikéyah *lies in the **Four Corners** region, where the corners of the present-day states of Utah, Colorado, Arizona, and New Mexico meet. The landscape is made up of deserts, canyons, mountains, and **mesas**. Mesas are raised tables of flat land. The **climate** of the* Diné Bikéyah *is very dry.*

A new way of life

Over time, the Athabascan speakers broke into several groups, including those now known as the Navajo and the Apache. The Navajo soon began meeting other Southwest nations, such as the nearby **Pueblo peoples**. From their Pueblo neighbors, the Navajo acquired new foods, clothing, and other goods. The Navajo and the Pueblo peoples also exchanged knowledge about hunting animals and raising crops that would grow in the region's dry climate.

Many changes

Spanish explorers arrived in the Southwest in the early 1600s. When they first encountered the Navajo people, they named them "Navajo," a Spanish word that meant "people with large fields." The Spaniards brought many changes to the Southwest. They introduced **domesticated** animals such as sheep, goats, and horses. The animals quickly became part of the Navajo people's daily lives (see pages 20-21).

The Navajo culture

This book describes the Navajo as they lived from 1700 until about 1850. Many Navajo people today have the same values, follow the same traditions, and hold the same beliefs as those described throughout the book.

Horses have been important to the Navajo since they were introduced in the 1600s.

*Navajo legends tell of giant birds that lived on Ship Rock. They hunted the Navajo until Monster Slayer, one of the **Holy People**, destroyed them and rescued their young—the eagles and owls of today.*

Harmony and respect

The beliefs of the Navajo—throughout history and today—have always been reflected in the daily lives of the people. The Navajo strive to maintain harmony, or *hózhǫ́*, among all living and nonliving things. They feel that if *hózhǫ́* is disrupted, bad fortune or illness may follow. To keep harmony, the Navajo treat people, plants, animals, and the land with respect. They follow traditional practices based on their beliefs. The Navajo people believe that they were created by the Holy People, or *Diyin Dine'é*, who inhabited the land before they did. The Holy People came to the *Diné Bikéyah* from the Underworlds and eventually gave the land to the Navajo. Knowledge of the Holy People is passed from parents and grandparents to children through an **oral tradition**, or a series of stories that describe the history, traditions, and beliefs of the Navajo culture. These stories are shared only between the first frost of autumn and the first thunder of spring.

Ceremonies

The Navajo today still practice many **rituals**, or traditional ceremonies, that were part of life in the past. Medicine men and women, known as *Hataałii*, perform the rituals from memory. They also teach them to young people. Rituals are performed at special times in a person's life. They often involve chants and **drypaintings**, shown left. Drypaintings are made using the colored powders of crushed rocks, charcoal, pollen, and cornmeal. The sacred patterns are passed from one **generation** to the next.

The Blessing Way ceremony is meant to bring good health and happiness to those who celebrate it.

The sacred *Diné Bikéyah*

The Navajo consider the *Diné Bikéyah* to be sacred because they believe the Holy People led the first Navajo people there long ago. The homeland lies amid four sacred mountains that have both Navajo and English names. They are Blanca Peak, or *Sis Naajiní*, in the east; Mount Taylor, or *Tsoodził*, in the south; San Francisco Mountain, or *Dook'o'oosłííd*, in the west; and Mount Hesperus, or *Dibe Nitsaa*, in the north. Within the boundaries of the *Diné Bikéyah*, there are other sacred mountains, including Huerfano Mountain, or *Dził Na'oodiłii*, and Gobernador Knob, or *Ch'ool'į́'į́*.

Navajo communities

Family has always been the foundation of the Navajo community. A basic family unit was made up of two parents and their unmarried children. A family usually lived near its **extended family**, or group of relations that included aunts, uncles, cousins, and grandparents. Together, the extended family formed a **local group**. They often lived close to one another in seasonal **camps** (see page 10). People were **seminomadic**, which means they moved from a winter settlement to a summer settlement. When the members of the camp moved, they usually stayed together.

The elders in a local group were very respected. People often asked for their guidance and advice.

The *Naat'áani*

Most of the time, a *Naat'áani*, or peace leader, looked out for the interests of a local group. All the men and women in the group had to agree when deciding who would act as their *Naat'áani*. The *Naat'áani* was a man to whom the community looked for guidance. He was a wise, well-spoken, and well-respected person who offered advice, settled disputes, and knew how ceremonies should be performed.

Task leaders

People who were skilled at specific tasks such as hunting, raids, healing ceremonies, and war could become temporary task leaders. These leaders had authority only in organizing and overseeing their own tasks, and their leadership lasted only as long as it took to complete their jobs. Leaders sometimes lost their power sooner, however, if people lost confidence in their leadership.

When big tasks such as gathering piñon nuts needed to be done, many people from a local group pitched in to share the work. They took turns working and resting in the shade.

Family life

Family camps were usually **matrilocal**, or made up of the homes of a mother and her daughters' families. When a young woman grew up and got married, she and her husband usually built a home close to her mother's home. Over time, camps could grow to include the homes of many families. The families worked together to provide for the whole camp. Resources such as food and clothing were shared or distributed by the **head mother**, who was the most respected mother in the camp. Everyone also pitched in to help with big jobs such as harvesting crops or herding animals. Each household relied on help from the camp in times of need.

Roles and duties

All family members had daily duties. Adults were responsible for maintaining their homes, tending animals, making clothing and other objects, and watching over children. They also made sure there was food for their households. Some hunted, some gathered wild plants, and others raised crops of grains and vegetables. Foods then had to be prepared for meals.

Older siblings looked after their younger brothers and sisters.

Part of a clan

Families are part of **clans**, or groups of extended families. The clans of the Navajo are **matrilineal**, which means that children are born into their mothers' clan. They grow up with strong ties to other clans, however, including the clan of their fathers. For example, the mother's clan is responsible for teaching a child to think and become aware of his or her surroundings. The father's clan teaches the child about the way the world works. By telling stories and sharing traditions, the **maternal** grandfather's clan teaches the child how to live in the Navajo way. The **paternal** grandfather's clan guides the child in prayer.

Marriage has always been an important part of Navajo life. According to oral tradition, Changing Woman, one of the Holy People, arranged the first marriages. She created four clans and made a brother and sister in each one. She then paired each sibling with a man or a woman from another clan. The couples were married by eating from a ceremonial basket, as shown right.

ceremonial basket

The tradition continues

The Navajo wedding ceremony developed from the marriage tradition. It took place in the home of the bride's mother. During the ceremony, the bride and groom washed each other's hands to represent starting fresh. They then ate cornmeal from a ceremonial basket. After the ceremony, a feast was held to celebrate the new couple.

Following the rules

There were rules about who could and could not get married. Two people who wanted to marry could not be related or belong to the same clan. In some areas, a man could have more than one wife. He might marry two sisters or a widow who needed someone to provide for her. No matter how many wives a man had, he was expected to join his new wife's family and help with tending flocks or raising crops.

The lives of children

Children were cared for by their parents and extended families. Almost all the local adults took part in raising and disciplining children. Some had special roles in children's lives. For example, the adult who made a baby laugh for the first time held a ceremony to celebrate the event, which represented prosperity, generosity, and good health. At the ceremony, people prayed that joy would always remain with the baby.

A Navajo child was known by many names during his or her lifetime. Parents gave every baby a sacred name as a source of power. The power was weakened each time the name was said aloud, so people did not use it every day. Instead, they referred to one another in terms of their relationship, such as "son of my sister." Children also became known by names that described what they looked like or their important accomplishments.

Work and play

Navajo children filled their days with many kinds of activities. Older children cared for and played with their younger brothers and sisters. They learned lessons in responsibility by caring for the family's animals and by helping with chores such as collecting firewood. They learned how to cook, hunt, and weave by watching their parents and other family members as they worked. The most gifted girls and boys learned sacred healing rituals.

When work was finished, children and adults alike found many ways to have fun. Stick-dice and string games, as well as foot races and horse races, were popular pastimes for people of all ages. Practical jokes were also part of daily life among Navajo families. Retelling oral traditions, a favorite winter pastime, helped children understand the history and culture of their people.

Safe and warm

The Navajo **cradleboard**, shown right, kept babies safe while they slept and while their mothers worked or traveled. Mothers wrapped babies in blankets and tied them gently but securely to the board using leather straps. The board had a footrest at the bottom and a canopy across the top to shade a baby's eyes. Every few hours, a mother took her baby out of the cradle so that he or she could move, play, and be cleaned.

At home in a hogan

A hogan's earth floor represents Mother Earth, and the rounded roof represents Father Sky.

Hogans, or *hooghan*, were the most common Navajo dwellings. These low clay-covered homes stayed warm in winter and cool in summer. Most families had hogans in more than one location, and they moved from one to another once or twice each year. Today, many Navajo people live in modern homes but have hogans nearby, in which they hold traditional ceremonies.

"Male" and "female" hogans

The earliest hogans were cone-shaped structures covered with earth. They had a framework of wooden poles that was covered with logs and brush and then packed with clay. These hogans are sometimes called "male" hogans. Around 1800, the Navajo began building hogans with six or more sides. They **cribbed**, or stacked, logs to form the walls and then packed mud over the rafters to build a roof. These hogans are known as "female" hogans.

Other structures

Most families had other buildings near their hogans. They stored extra belongings in **dugouts** and worked under the shade of **ramadas,** or open-sided structures made of four poles and a **thatched** roof. **Sweat lodges** were low airtight structures that were warmed with heated rocks. When the lodges grew hot, people sat inside and sweated to bathe themselves. Sweat baths were often accompanied by rituals and songs.

"male" hogan

Inside the hogan

A fire in the middle of the floor kept the whole hogan warm. A hole in the roof allowed sunlight to enter and smoke to escape. Prayers were also thought to leave through the hole. People slept on sheep skins on the ground. They hung belongings from the rafters or stored them in baskets. Everyone had his or her own "spot" inside the hogan. Men usually stayed on the south side, whereas women kept to the north side. The west side was reserved for the most honored person in the hogan, such as a guest or a family elder. When entering a hogan, people moved in a circular, "sunwise" path. From the door, they moved south, west, and then north to reach their spots.

*The Navajo believe that the Holy People built the first hogans using materials such as **turquoise** and shell. Many people place pieces of these materials under the poles of their hogans. The hogans are always built with the doorway facing east, in the direction of the rising sun.*

Food from the land

The *Diné Bikéyah* provided the Navajo with plenty of food. Despite the dry climate, many kinds of plants and animals lived there. Gatherers searched for wild berries, seeds, herbs, and fruits from cactus plants and different types of trees. Animals such as rabbits, deer, mountain goats, and prairie dogs were common **game**, or animals to hunt. Before each hunt, the hunters performed rituals and thanked the animals that would provide food for their families. Hunters and gatherers often had to travel long distances to find the foods they needed.

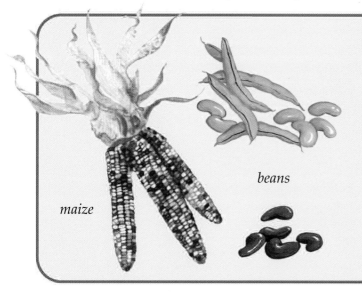

maize

beans

Growing crops

The Navajo people raised crops of **maize**, or corn, as well as beans, squash, and fruits such as peaches. The harvests from these crops helped round out a diet of meat and wild plants. Most Navajo farmers were **flood farmers**. They planted their crops in areas that were flooded by rainfall or overflowing rivers. They could farm only during the summer months, when floods came.

Respect for the land

The Navajo depended on the land for their survival and worked hard to keep a balance between themselves and the plants and animals on which they relied. Hunters did not **overhunt**, or kill more animals than they needed for their survival. They did not hunt certain creatures, including coyotes, snakes, and eagles, because they believed these animals were sacred.

eagle

coyote

snake

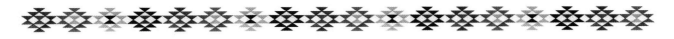

Delicious dishes

Navajo people passed on the art of cooking from one generation to the next. They did not write down recipes. Instead, adults worked with children to prepare meals, teaching as they worked. Cooks measured ingredients with their hands and fingers. Most meals were cooked over a fire, either outside or in the center of the hogan. Cooking pots and tools were stored near the fire pit and were cleaned and stored after meals were finished.

Favorite foods, such as ground cake and kneel-down bread, were made with maize.

The importance of animals

When the Spaniards arrived in the early 1600s, they brought domesticated animals with them. These animals, especially horses, sheep, and goats, quickly became an important part of Navajo life.

A mobile lifestyle

Dibé, or sheep and goats, provided fleece, meat, and milk. Many Navajo families raised **mixed flocks**, or flocks made up of both sheep and goats. When a season was over or when grass or water became scarce, people packed up their camps. They took their flocks and went in search of a new spot with plentiful resources.

Swift horses

Horses became important to the Navajo because they made the transportation of people and goods easier and faster. People could cover long distances more quickly on horseback than they could on foot. Horses enabled people to visit and stay in touch with distant relatives more easily. People also rode horses to look for new grazing lands or to reach distant places where certain wild plants and animals lived.

Sheep, goats, and horses were very important to the livelihood of the Navajo. People took excellent care of their animals and taught their children to do the same.

A new economy

The Navajo raised sheep mainly for their fleece, which people spun into wool yarn. The yarn was then woven into blankets and cloth that was used to make clothing and other items.

Wool provided the Navajo with so many valuable things that their livelihood was soon based on sheep. A family with a large flock of sheep was considered wealthy. Less wealthy families had smaller flocks or helped raise the flocks of their relatives.

Weaving

The Navajo people were weavers even before Spaniards brought sheep to the Southwest. They used fibers from wild plants such as wild cotton and yucca to create blankets, mats, and cloth.

On a loom

Once domesticated sheep became more common, Navajo weavers began using wool instead of plant fibers. The neighboring Pueblo peoples wove fibers on **looms**, or wooden frames. The Navajo soon made looms like those of the Pueblo peoples, but their weaving style was different. Some historians believe that it is more like the style of the Navajo's Athabascan ancestors. Today, Navajo weaving is a highly prized Southwestern art form. Blankets and **tapestries** with traditional bold diamond and zigzag patterns are in demand all over the world.

Navajo blankets provided protection from wind and cold temperatures. They also made comfortable bedding. They could even be made into simple dresses (see page 24). Blankets could also be tied into bundles and used to carry objects. Some people placed blankets under saddles to protect the skin of horses.

Making blankets

Depending on its size, a single blanket could take up to 200 hours to weave! The intricate patterns and the many colors used to make different blankets meant that weavers had to spend a great deal of time planning their designs and preparing wool. Designs came from each weaver's imagination. Early blankets were made with off-white, gray, or brown wool that was taken from the light- and dark-colored sheep in the flock. Before long, however, weavers began to dye the fibers. They used plants such as piñon trees and rabbitweed to make dyes of different shades. Weavers also traded for a Spanish fabric called **bayeta**, a soft red cloth, which they unraveled in order to use its richly colored thread.

serape, or shoulder blanket

Spider Woman
In a traditional legend, the Navajo tell how the craft of weaving was given to them by Spider Woman, one of the Holy People. Weavers believe that they must leave a "way out" of the blanket so that their creativity and energy can move on to other projects once the blanket is completed. Early blankets each had a hole in the center, but later blankets usually incorporated the way out into the pattern. It usually moves from the center to the right edge, toward the "south" of the blanket.

Spider Woman's home is said to be on top of Spider Rock in Arizona's Canyon de Chelly.

Arts, crafts, and clothing

Baskets are woven with patterns that represent important ideas. Elders often use baskets to tell stories, tracing the patterns with their fingers as they speak.

Navajo people had to make all the everyday objects they needed. To make these goods, they collected natural materials such as animal hides, plant fibers, and minerals. The goods could be kept for the family or traded for other items. By trading with other nations, people were able to get materials that were not found near their homes or goods that they did not make themselves. Navajo hunters, for example, traded meat and animal hides with Pueblo farmers, who had a variety of vegetables, fruits, and grains to offer in exchange.

Clothing

The earliest Navajo people wore clothing and shoes called moccasins that were made of **buckskin**, or deer hide. Women wore buckskin dresses and men wore buckskin shirts, leggings, and breechcloths, or coverings worn around the waist. Over time, people began making their clothing from woven cloth, and styles began to change. People started wearing decorative blankets and sashes, which were beautiful as well as useful. Women began making dresses similar to those worn by Pueblo women. The dresses were made from two blankets fastened over the shoulder. Men began wearing buckskin pants instead of leggings. People also knitted wool garments. They used slender branches to make smooth, hard knitting needles.

Silversmiths

Starting in the early 1600s, the Navajo traded for silver with the Spaniards and the Mexicans, but they did not begin to make their own silver objects until later. They learned from Mexican silversmiths called *plateros* how to melt down silver coins and use them to make rings, beads, buttons, buckles, pins, bells, and other useful, beautiful objects. They often **inlaid**, or set, shaped pieces of turquoise to add color and decoration to silver objects. Today, Navajo silver jewelry is well known and prized around the world.

Dangerous times

King Philip II ruled Spain from 1556 to 1598. In 1583, he issued a royal decree calling for a wealthy Spanish man to lead the effort to settle the Southwest region.

The Navajo became skilled riders and were soon able to use horses to improve their chances in battle against the Spaniards.

The arrival of Spanish explorers in the Southwest brought some positive changes to the lives of the Navajo people, but it also created many problems. Along with useful things such as sheep and horses, the Spaniards brought many dangers. They also tried to force changes upon the Navajo and other Southwest nations. When the nations resisted the changes, violence broke out.

Imported dangers

The Spaniards brought weapons, especially firearms, that were new to the Native people. Firearms made warfare between Spanish soldiers and Native people more deadly than any fighting the Native groups had experienced before. The Spanish also traded alcohol with the Native people, which caused many problems, including sickness. The most dangerous import, however, was disease. Contagious diseases such as influenza and small pox were new to the Native people, and their bodies had no defense against them. Millions of Native people were killed by the new diseases.

Owning land

The Navajo believed that land could not be owned by any one person. The Spanish explorers, however, claimed the land for the King of Spain. In turn, the king granted plots of land to his subjects.

Owning people

Spanish settlers not only claimed land, they also claimed the Navajo people who were living on it. They forced the Navajo to become **slaves**. The Spanish forced more Navajo into slavery than any other Native group in the Southwest. Some Navajo people had slaves of their own, but they usually treated the slaves as members of their households. The Spaniards, however, were not as kind to their slaves. They often traded Navajo slaves to Mexican miners, who forced the slaves into hard labor. Trading slaves was so profitable that Spanish traders often kidnapped Navajo people and sold them into slavery. Navajo groups sometimes launched raids against the Spanish settlers to fight back against these kidnappings.

*The Navajo and other Southwest Native people were often forced to build **missions**. The people who belonged to these religious communities believed that they could make the Native people give up their own beliefs and become Christians.*

Forced change

The American government acquired the Southwest in 1848 after the Mexican-American War ended. The *Diné Bikéyah* had many natural resources, including coal and oil, which the government wanted. Before long, the government began offering the Navajo **treaties**, or agreements, that would take away parts of the *Diné Bikéyah*. The land was sacred to the Navajo, so they resisted signing these treaties and giving up their land. In the 1850s, the U.S. government built a fort in the middle of the *Diné Bikéyah*. They named it Fort Defiance. The Navajo began fighting for their land. The government decided that the Navajo should be moved to Fort Sumner, or *Hwéeldi*, many miles away. Colonel Kit Carson forced the Navajo people to move by destroying hogans, burning crops, killing animals, and poisoning water supplies. Before long, it was impossible for the Navajo to survive on their land.

Arthur Shilstone

The Long Walk

Driven from their homes, many Navajo people were forced to make the **Long Walk** to Fort Sumner. The 400 mile (644 km) walk took place in the winter of 1864. Many people froze, starved, became ill, or were shot to death along the way. Some escaped during the journey, but most escapees were caught and killed by soldiers or kidnapped by Mexican slave traders. The survivors arrived at Fort Sumner, where they had to crowd onto about 40 square miles (104 km²) of land—only a fraction of the size of the *Diné Bikéyah*.

Fort Sumner

There was no natural shelter at Fort Sumner, and people did not have the materials to make hogans. They had to build makeshift homes by digging holes in the ground and covering them with brush and cloth. The army gave out blankets, but they were so thin that Navajo weavers had to unravel and reweave them into thicker fabric. Crops failed year after year, and many people starved to death. As many as 9,000 Navajo people lived in the small area, and diseases spread quickly because of the overcrowded conditions.

Going home

In 1868, the Navajo were finally released from Fort Sumner. A treaty was signed that allowed the people to return to a parcel of land on the *Diné Bikéyah*, but this area was only about one-tenth of the original size of their homeland. In June of 1868, a line of Navajo more than ten miles (16 km) long set out for the new **reservation** in the *Diné Bikéyah*.

The Navajo today

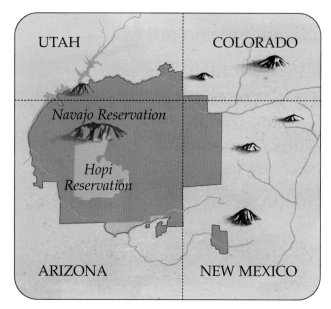

A reservation for the Hopi people of the Southwest lies within the boundaries of the Navajo Reservation.

Today, there are 290,000 members of the Navajo nation living in the United States. Many live on the Navajo Reservation. Since 1868, land has been added to the original reservation in order to accommodate the growing population. The reservation now covers about 25,000 square miles (64 750 km²) of land.

Keeping a culture alive

Navajo culture continues to thrive in the Southwest. Scholars teach Navajo history, culture, and language to both Navajo and non-Navajo people at Diné College. Navajo radio stations, television stations, and newspapers keep people informed in the Navajo language.

A self-governed people

The Navajo nation today has its own government system in addition to the traditional organization of families and local groups. This government represents the Navajo people as part of the United States. A **judicial**, or court, system called the Courts of the Navajo Nation helps enforce laws based on the American legal system. In addition, the Navajo Peacemaker Court allows Navajo people to settle disputes based on the principles of the traditional *Naat'áani* leadership.

Many Navajo artists, including this weaver, honor their heritage in beautiful works of art.

Learn more!

There are several terrific websites that offer information on the rich history, culture, art, and language of the Navajo people. Learn more by visiting these sites:

- www.westernindian.org/navajo_history_culture.htm
- www.americanwest.com/pages/navajo2.htm
- www.navajocentral.org

Code talkers

During World War II, the United States Marine Corps recruited about 400 Navajo soldiers to deliver secret messages in the Navajo language. Code breakers in the opposing forces tried to decode these messages to learn the locations of troops, ships, and submarines. The code breakers were never able to decode the Navajo messages, however, which helped save many American soldiers. The service of the Navajo code talkers was recognized in 2001, when they were awarded Gold and Silver Congressional Medals of Honor.

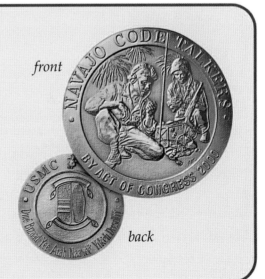

front

back

Glossary

Note: Boldfaced terms that are defined in the text may not appear in the glossary.

ancestor A relative from long ago

camp A group of semi-permanent dwellings

clan A group of extended families that are related to one another

climate The long-term weather patterns of an area

domesticated Describing animals that are raised by humans and are used to living near them

dugout A shelter or storage space made by digging a hole in the ground

generation A group of people who are roughly the same age

Holy People The figures in the Navajo tradition who brought the Navajo people to their homeland

hunter-gatherer A person who hunts animals and collects plant foods to survive

local group A group of relatives living in one area

maternal Describing that which belongs to the family line of a mother

mission A religious community built in order to convert Native people to Christianity

nation A group of Native people with a common language, culture, and history

nomadic Describing people who do not settle in one place but constantly move from one location to another

oral tradition The stories and songs passed from one generation to the next as a way of sharing history, culture, and values

paternal Describing that which belongs to the family line of a father

Pueblo peoples The Native peoples of the Southwest known for living in apartment-style stone or adobe structures called pueblos

reservation A parcel of government land set aside for Native people

ritual A traditional set of actions and words performed to achieve a desired result, such as healing or success in hunting

seminomadic Describing people who stay in a settlement for only part of the year

slave A person who is forced to work without being paid for his or her labor

tapestry A woven cloth with a design

thatched Describing an object that is made by weaving grasses and brush

turquoise A type of blue-green stone

Index